Shop 'Til You Drop

by
David Orme

Thunderbolts

Shop 'Til You Drop
by David Orme

Illustrated by Demitri The Krah

Published by Ransom Publishing Ltd.
Radley House, 8 St. Cross Road, Winchester, Hants. SO23 9HX, UK
www.ransom.co.uk

ISBN   978 178127 065 3
First published in 2013
Reprinted 2023

Copyright © 2013 Ransom Publishing Ltd.

Illustrations copyright © 2013 Demitri The Krah
'Get the Facts' section - images copyright: cover, prelims, passim – Marieke Kuijjer, David Orme, Benh Lieu Song; pp 8/9 - Christian Frausto Bernal, Dungodung, Mark.murphy, David Orme; pp 10/11 - Waggers, gilles lougassi, Natalia Silych; pp 12/13 - Helen Orme, Catherine Yeulet; pp 14/15 - Marieke Kuijjer, istolethetv, Biswarup Ganguly; pp 16/17 - Jakub Kalaska, Cihcvlss, Edward, 293.xx.xxx.xx; pp 18/19 - konradlew, 11860951, Alexander Novikov, JJ Harrison, Jan Kameníček, Ronald Saunders; pp 20/21 - Cmglee, Heng Kong Chen, Electroliner, Kangxi emperor6868; pp 22/23 - FernandoAH, Bogdan Kosanovic, PeskyMonkey; p 36 - Laszlo Ilyes.

A CIP catalogue record of this book is available from the British Library.

All rights reserved. No part of this publication may be reproduced, stored in a retrieval system, or transmitted, in any form or by any means, electronic, mechanical, photocopying, recording or otherwise, without the prior permission of the publishers.

The rights of David Orme to be identified as the author and of Demitri The Krah to be identified as the illustrator of this Work have been asserted by them in accordance with sections 77 and 78 of the Copyright, Design and Patents Act 1988.

Contents

Shop 'Til You Drop: The Facts   5

'It's Got to Go Back'   25

Shop 'Til You Drop: The Facts

In the past

Alabama USA, 1937

Butcher's stall, 1550

Markets

Clothes market

Food market

Car boot sale

Indoor market

Deliveries – then and now

Food shops – then and now

Grocer, 1930s

The first supermarket – 1917

Eat on the street!

Street food in India

Scorpions and starfish: China

Yum!

15

How much do you want to spend?

Buy a car – £1,100

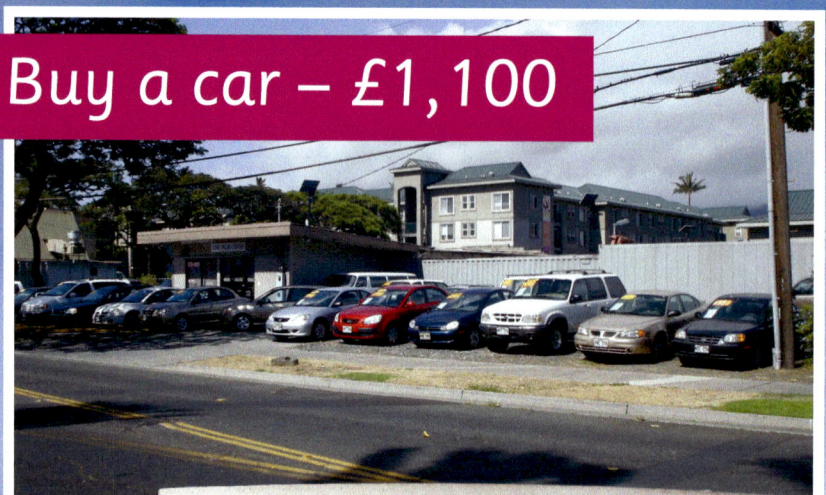

Buy a car – £300,000

Buy a bag – £1

Buy a bag – £12,000

Shopper's calendar

Which is which?

Summer

Halloween

Easter

Mother's day

Christmas

19

Shopping malls

Is this the Pyramids?
No, it's a shopping mall.

Is this Italy? No, it's a shopping mall.

Shopping online is easy!

Josh and Matt are out shopping …

… but they don't have any money.

Back at home ...

Big sister Liz has found it!

Josh is too scared to do it …

BLEEP

The police are on their way.

Liz is in trouble …

Josh to the rescue ...

"It was me!"

34

Mum and Dad arrive. Josh is in **BIG** trouble!

Word list

butcher
calendar
China
christmas
clothes
deliveries
food
halloween
India
indoor
Italy
mall
market
money
mother's day
Pyramids
Rome
scorpion
shop
shopper
spend
starfish
street
summer
supermarket
trouble